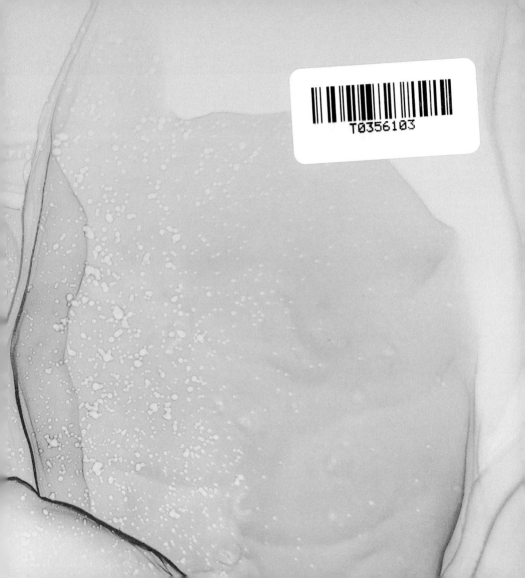

T0356103

LITTLE BOOK OF

Inspiration

Keepsake Gift Book

A Gift For:

_____

From:

_____

A bird doesn't sing because it has an answer, it sings because it has a song.

—MAYA ANGELOU

Maya Angelou (1928–2014) was an American poet, civil rights activist, memoirist, and a Renaissance woman who inspired generations. She won the Presidential Medal of Freedom in 2010, which is the highest civilian honor in the U.S.

The way to get started is to quit talking and begin doing.

—WALT DISNEY

Walt Disney (1901–1966), founder of The Disney Company, was a visionary and pioneer of animated cartoons and theme parks. He created beloved characters like Mickey Mouse, Donald Duck, and more that will be known for the rest of time.

I know it's cliché, but this is so true, you are the captain of your own ship; don't let anyone else take the wheel. Design life for yourself, you won't receive a second opportunity to do so, so you either do it now, or you regret it later on in life.

—STEVE JOBS

Steve Jobs (1955–2011) was a renowned inventor who cofounded Apple. He is credited for revolutionizing personal computers and leading the development of iconic consumer technology, like the iPhone, used by over a billion people every single day.

The future belongs to those who believe in the beauty of their dreams.

—ELEANOR ROOSEVELT

Eleanor Roosevelt (1884–1962) was the longest serving First Lady of the United States alongside her husband, Franklin D. Roosevelt, from 1933–1945. During her time in office, she redefined the role of First Lady with her public engagement and impactful advocacy.

Keep your face always toward the sunshine,
and shadows will fall behind you.

—WALT WHITMAN

Walt Whitman (1819–1892) was an American poet, essayist, and journalist known for incorporating transcendentalism and realism into his writing. He's often regarded as the father of free verse and is considered one of the most influential poets in American literature.

Your self worth is determined by you. You don't have to depend on someone telling you who you are.

—BEYONCÉ

Beyoncé Knowles-Carter is a singer, songwriter, actress, and one of the world's most famous performers. As of 2024, she holds the record for most Grammy Awards in history at 23 wins and counting.

Remember that hope is a powerful weapon even when all else is lost.

—NELSON MANDELA

Nelson Mandela (1918–2013) was a leader of the African National Congress liberation movement, spending 27 years in prison opposing South Africa's apartheid system. He was awarded the Nobel Peace Prize in 1993 and served as President of South Africa from 1994–1999.

If you don't like the road you're walking, start paving another one.

—DOLLY PARTON

Dolly Parton is a singer-songwriter, philanthropist, and country music icon who pioneered the blending of country and pop music styles. In November 2024, *Billboard* named Dolly the greatest country artist of all time.

If you're lucky enough to be different, never change.

—TAYLOR SWIFT

Taylor Swift is a global superstar and one of the most influential artists in contemporary music known for her songwriting, versatility, and cultural impact. In 2024, she broke the world record for highest grossing concert tour with her iconic *Eras Tour*

For me, I am driven by two main philosophies: know more today about the world than I knew yesterday, and lessen the suffering of others. You'd be surprised how far that gets you.

—NEIL DEGRASSE TYSON

Neil DeGrasse Tyson is an astrophysicist, author, television host, and science communicator famous for popularizing astrophysical concepts and discoveries. In 2017, he was awarded the Public Welfare Medal by the U.S. National Academy of Sciences for his role in exciting the world about the wonders of science.

Not all of us can do great things, but we can do small things with great love.

—MOTHER TERESA

Mother Teresa (1910–1997) is best known for founding the Missionaries of Charity, a religious order that provides aid to the poor, sick, and destitute. In 1979, she was awarded the Nobel Peace Prize for her humanitarian work and in 2016 was declared a Saint by Pope Francis.

It has always been easy to hate and destroy.
To build and to cherish is much more difficult.

—QUEEN ELIZABETH II

Queen Elizabeth II (1926–2022) is known for being the longest-reigning monarch in British history, serving from 1952 until her death in 2022. She is credited with modernizing the monarchy, raising over $2 billion for nonprofits including climate change, education, and healthcare.

Travel changes you. As you move through this life and this world you change things slightly, you leave marks behind, however small. And in return, life—and travel—leaves marks on you.

—ANTHONY BOURDAIN

We have to make the choice—every single day—to exemplify the truth, the respect, and the grace that we wish for this world.

—OPRAH WINFREY

Oprah Winfrey is a television icon, TV host, actress, a media mogul, and philanthropist, launching her own television network, the Oprah Winfrey Network (OWN), in 2011. Oprah started the Oprah's Angel Network in 1998, dedicated to supporting charitable projects around the world.

I don't know anything with certainty,
but seeing the stars makes me dream.

—VINCENT VAN GOGH

Vincent van Gogh (1853–1890) is celebrated as one of the most influential and popular Postimpressionist painters of his time, known for his expressive use of color, textured brushwork, and profound connection to nature and the human experience.

*The time is always right to
do what is right.*

—MARTIN LUTHER KING, JR.

Martin Luther King, Jr. (1929–1968) was a prominent African American leader in the civil rights movement of the 50s and 60s. He was an inspirational speaker, delivering his most famous speech, "I Have a Dream," in 1963, which continues to inspire millions around the world of all ages, winning the Nobel Peace Prize in 1964.

Don't make your career be your life. Let it be your passion. Let it bring you pleasure. But don't let it become your identity. You are so much more valuable than that.

—CELINE DION

Celine Dion is known as the "queen of power ballads," selling over 200 million albums worldwide, and winning five Grammy Awards. She is recognized as the best-selling French language artist of all time.

One child, one teacher, one book, one pen can change the world.

—MALALA YOUSAFZAI

Malala Yousafzai is a Pakistani activist and 2014 Nobel Peace Prize winner. She is a fierce women's advocate, fighting to promote girls' education and children's rights. At age 19, in 2017, she was appointed as the youngest-ever United Nations Messenger of Peace.

Humans only have one ending.
Ideas live forever.

—GRETA GERWIG

Greta Gerwig is an actress, playwright, screenwriter, and director. Greta's 2023 film
Barbie® was the highest-grossing movie of all time by a solo female director.

If there is no struggle, there is no progress.

—FREDERICK DOUGLASS

Frederick Douglass (1818–1895) was an author, a leader of the abolitionist movement, and a champion of human rights for all. He is considered the father the civil rights movement, advising Presidents Abraham Lincoln and Andrew Johnson about Black suffrage.

There's really no point in asking: what if? The only question worth asking is: what's next?

—ELTON JOHN

Elton John, a British singer, songwriter, pianist, and multi-Grammy-winning legend, is one of the most successful and high-acclaimed musicians of all time. In 1992, he founded the Elton John AIDS Foundation, which has raised over £300 million since its inception.

Everything requires discipline, hard work, and dedication and, most importantly, self-belief.

—SERENA WILLIAMS

Serena Williams is one of the most powerful women's tennis players of all time, winning 23 Grand Slam single titles, more than any other woman in the Open Era. She is the second-most-decorated female Olympic tennis player after her older sister, Venus Williams, with four gold medals.

*I have no special talents. I am
only passionately curious.*

—ALBERT EINSTEIN

Albert Einstein (1879–1955) is recognized for his revolutionary work in physics, including the development of the theory of relativity (including e=mc²) and the photoelectric effect, which earned him a Nobel Prize in 1921.

*What you do makes a difference,
and you have to decide what kind
of difference you want to make.*

—DR. JANE GOODALL

Dr. Jane Goodall is an ethologist and conservationist whose work with chimpanzees has changed how people understand the relationship between humans and animals. She won the Templeton Prize in 2021 for her commitment to her groundbreaking discoveries.

I love the fact that I can make people happy, in any form. Even if it's just an hour of their lives, if I can make them feel lucky, or make them feel good, or bring a smile to a sour face, that to me is worthwhile.

—FREDDIE MERCURY

Freddie Mercury (1946–1991) was a singer-songwriter and lead singer of Queen, whose music reached the top of the U.S. and British charts in the 70s and 80s and continues to inspire new generations of listeners. He is remembered as one of the greatest singers in history.

I feel like if you're a really good human being, you can try to find something beautiful in every single person, no matter what.

—LADY GAGA

Lady Gaga is a singer-songwriter and pop icon, famously known for her strong vocals, flamboyant costumes, and provocative vocals. In 2012, she founded a nonprofit called the Born This Way Foundation, which supports mental wellness in people struggling with their mental health.

I can accept failure, everyone fails at something. But I can't accept not trying.

—MICHAEL JORDAN

Michael Jordan is one of the most decorated athletes in history and is considered one of the greatest basketball players of all time, winning six NBA championships. Michael is a five-time MVP, a 14-time All Star, and he won Rookie of the Year in 1985.

No matter what people tell you, words and ideas can change the world.

—ROBIN WILLIAMS

Robin Williams (1951–2014), a drama and comedy actor known for his improvisational skills, endless characters, and lovable personality, is regarded as one of the greatest comedians of all time.

Nothing is absolute. Everything changes,
everything moves, everything revolves,
everything flies and goes away.

—FRIDA KAHLO

Frida Kahlo (1907–1954) is famously known for her portrait paintings and is
celebrated for her attention to Mexican and Indigenous culture.

*Even if you are not ready for day,
it cannot always be night.*

—GWENDOLYN BROOKS

Gwendolyn Brooks (1917–2000), an author and poet, was the first African American to win the Pulitzer Prize for poetry in 1950 for her book *Annie Allen*, and she was the first African American woman to be inducted to the American Academy of Arts and Letters in 1976.

Don't try to be young. Just open your mind. Stay interested in stuff. There are so many things I won't live long enough to find out about, but I'm still curious about them.

—BETTY WHITE

Images from Shutterstock.com: Smileus (Cover, 11); Olga Popova (2, 10, 22, 32, 60); Kanyshev Andrey (3); spatuletail (3, 14, 30, 40, 46, 48, 50, 58); Kemarrravv13 (6); Repina Valeriya (7); MM_photos (8); ClaudiaRamirezValdespino (9); Tinseltown (12, 34); IS MODE (13); Manzooranmai (15); Kathy Hutchins (16, 20, 26, 42); Bob Pool (17); DFree (18, 36, 38, 52); Melinda Nagy (19); sripfoto (21); ju_see (23); Alessia Pierdomenico (24); Stacey Ann Alberts (25); Andrew Mayovskyy (27, 53); Maxim Elramisisy (28); Anna Ok (29); Body Stock (33); Gorodenkoff (35); Mariana Serdynska (37); icemanphotos (39); Claus Mikosch (41); Maliutina Anna (43); Kim Yuk Hyun (45); jag_cz (47); xilonm (49); Avis De Miranda (51); landmarkmedia (54); Pikoso.kz (55); Vicki L. Miller (56); biletskiyevgeniy (57); Nejron Photo (59); OlegRi (61); s_buckley (62); ANNA TITOVA (63).

Images from Alamy.com: sunflower6000 (5); Zoonar GmbH (31).

ISBN 978-1-4971-0556-0

Library of Congress Control Number: 2024925895

To learn more about the other great books from Fox Chapel Publishing, or to find a retailer near you, call toll-free 800-457-9112, or visit us at www.FoxChapelPublishing.com.

You can also send mail to:
903 Square Street
Mount Joy, PA 17552.

We are always looking for talented authors. To submit an idea, please send a brief inquiry to acquisitions@foxchapelpublishing.com.

Printed in China

First printing

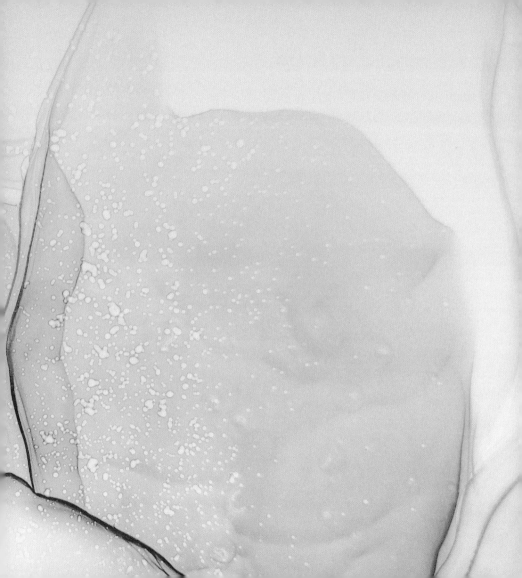